MUSINGS OF A 90s BABY

VERSES OF DARKNESS, DREAMS & DAWN

Mohak Suri

First published in 2026

Copyright © Mohak Suri, 2026

ISBN: 978-93-5717-623-1

TABLE OF CONTENTS

DEDICATION..7

PREFACE..9

ACKNOWLEDGMENTS..11

VERSE 1...12

VERSE 2...16

VERSE 3...20

VERSE 4...24

VERSE 5...28

VERSE 6...32

VERSE 7...36

VERSE 8...38

VERSE 9...42

VERSE 10..46

VERSE 11..50

VERSE 12..54

VERSE 13..58

VERSE 14..62

VERSE 15..66

VERSE 16..70

VERSE 17..74

VERSE 18..78

VERSE 19..82

VERSE 20...86

VERSE 21...90

VERSE 22...94

VERSE 23...98

VERSE 24..102

VERSE 25..106

VERSE 26..110

VERSE 27..114

VERSE 28..118

VERSE 29..122

VERSE 30..126

ABOUT THE AUTHOR 139

<u>DEDICATION</u>

To the 90s babies who grew up between cable TV and streaming,
who learned patience waiting for screens to buffer or dreams to stick.
To those who still search for connection in a sea of people,
who carry yesterday's nostalgia and tomorrow's hope in equal parts.
To anyone who's ever talked to themselves and called it a conversation,
who's still searching for their way in this world.
If you've known dark nights, chased after dreams,
or just waited for light to break –
These verses hold our truths.

PREFACE

I've been writing poetry nearly my entire life – not to get noticed or win applause, but because I needed it.
When words failed me in conversation, when trusting someone felt too risky, the written word became my sanctuary. It's where I didn't have to hold back, where I could scream into the void and hear my own echo.

For years, these poems lived hidden away in notebook scraps and text files on my computer, meant only for my eyes.
They were mine alone – the raw, unfiltered fragments of my soul trying to navigate a world that moves too fast, and doesn't always care. But at some point, something changed. Maybe I just got tired of hiding. Maybe I found a bit of courage I didn't know I had.

This collection isn't some perfect, polished thing. It's darkness I've survived, dreams I've clung to, and dawns I've waited for. It's the story of a 90s kid looking for a place to belong, figuring out a voice that feels like his own, and finding a path that makes sense.

If even one person reads these verses and feels a little less alone in their own struggle, then sharing this part of my soul will have been worth it.

THESE POEMS ARE MY TRUTH. NOW, THEY'RE YOURS TOO.

ACKNOWLEDGMENTS

To the storytellers – the writers, musicians, filmmakers, and creators whose work shaped my growing years and made my solitude feel less empty. You showed me that words could carry weight, how feelings can be transformed into art, and that it's okay to feel everything, even when it's overwhelming. Thank you for teaching a quiet kid that being vulnerable is its own kind of strength.

To my friends – the ones who've stuck with me through the chaos, the ones I've lost along the way, and the ones whose stories will someday intertwine with mine.
Every conversation, every comfortable shared silence, all the laughter and tears – you're all in these pages. You've left your mark on my being, whether you know it or not.

And to my mother – my friend, my rock, my unwavering constant in a world that never stops spinning. Thank you for your patience with my silences, for believing in me even when I struggled to believe in myself, and for giving me the space to become who I needed to be. This wouldn't exist without you.

VERSE 1

Growing up as the quiet, bullied kid meant every team selection during playtime was a fresh humiliation.
I was the one always picked last, the one even the bullied would bully in turn.
Recess wasn't freedom; it was a reminder of invisibility.

But after school, in the glow of a screen with a controller in hand, there was refuge.

This poem is about that childhood isolation and the refuge found in video games and stories – worlds where you could be the hero instead of the afterthought, where solitude felt like choice rather than rejection.

THE LAST ONE LEFT

They chose their teams like picking fruit from trees,
The ripest first, the strongest, the sweetest catch.
I stood there waiting, rooted in unease,
The last one left, the burden, the losing match.

Recess wasn't freedom's call or a child's joy,
But sixty minutes of torture dressed as playtime.
I'd find the shadows, become the quiet boy,
And count the seconds till the bell would chime.

They'd laugh and shove and trip me in the halls,
Their cruelty a game they played with ease.
I'd pick myself up from those countless falls,
And learn that asking why brought no release.

Even the outcasts found someone to scorn,
Someone weaker they could push aside.
A chain of cruelty, link by link was worn,
And I was at the end with nowhere left to hide.

When three o'clock arrived, I'd rush outside,
The journey home a countdown to relief.
I'd shut the world away and run to hide
In places that would understand my grief.

A controller resting warm in my hands,
A story waiting that offered me escape.
In pixelated far-off distant lands,
I wasn't picked last – I could choose my fate.

No ritual humiliation every day,
No corners where I'd hide and disappear.
In digital escapes I'd find my way,
A chosen one, a hero without peer.

The empty slot for player two remained,
A reminder that I still played alone.
But here the loneliness felt less like pain,
At least these worlds could feel a bit like home.

VERSE 2

Not all love gets spoken aloud.

This poem captures the weight of a secret crush—
the person whose kindness made unbearable days
survivable, whose friendship I treasured too much to
gamble on a confession of feelings.

It's about unrequited love at a young age, about how the
smallest moments of connection can mean everything.

It's about the bittersweet beauty of that unrequited love,
where friendship is both salvation and silent heartbreak
wrapped into one.

A JAR OF BUTTERFLIES

She carried grace I couldn't comprehend,
The prettiest soul I'd come to know.
And somehow, impossibly to me,
She offered friendship's gentle glow.

I never told her what my heart would say,
The words stayed locked behind my careful smile.
I'd see her coming and I'd lose my way,
My gut, a jar of butterflies, alive and wild.

Each time we talked became a treasured thing,
The highlight that would brighten up my day.
Her laughter was a melody to which I'd cling,
It held me when the world all turned to gray.

She didn't know the weight her kindness held,
How precious every moment felt to me.
I kept my feelings locked, my courage scattered,
Too afraid of what would cease to be.

So I stayed quiet, treasured what we had,
Each conversation, every small shared thing.
I swallowed my feelings, bittersweet and sad,
And wore my friendship like a sheltering wing.

Each little moment meant the world to me,
A shared joke, walking down the road.
My friendship was the only part set free,
My love stayed locked in its dark abode.

Then life brought distance neither could prevent,
I moved away, the distance between us wide.
Before lives were lived through glowing screens,
Across the void, our kinship died.

Some love stays buried, never finds its voice,
A bittersweet feeling that lingers through the years.
She gave me light through friendship by her choice,
And loving her in silence felt most fair.

I wonder if she knows what she once meant,
To someone who loved silently back then.
Who cherished every moment that was spent,
A live jar of butterflies, now and again.

VERSE 3

Some wounds never get names. Some scars are carved too deep to show.

This poem's about any and all trauma that is experienced by many a person in their teens but is never spoken aloud – Not to family, not to therapists, not to anyone.

It's about hurt inflicted by people who should have been safe, by multiple hands in multiple places, each one adding to a burden one can never truly set down.
It's about the silence that becomes survival, the way you learn to lock things away in sealed up boxes in dark corners of yourself just to keep functioning.

It's about carrying those boxes into your twenties, your thirties, feeling its weight but never opening them up again. It's about memories that ambush you decades later, and the realization that some secrets might never be safe to tell.

SEALED UP BOXES

Some things are never said aloud, wounds that never get their name,
Scars that live deep beneath the skin where nobody can see them.
Some hands that should have kept you safe instead inflicted shame,
Secrets carved into your bones, too heavy to relieve them.
Stacked like boxes in the darkness, each one bearing different stain,
Sealed away forever, never to be opened again.

So you build yourself a system, lock each memory away,
Seal the boxes tight with nails, refuse to look inside.
Since your teens you've been running, avoiding them even today,
Still they follow everywhere, no matter where you hide.
Some burdens never lighten, never fade as decades pass,
Simply settle in your bones and make their home at last.

Some days the words rise up like bile, threatening your throat,
Surfacing like poison that you have to swallow down.
Still you never tell a soul, never seek a therapist's note,
Speaking them could crumble every wall you've built around.
So silence is the armor that you chose to wear instead,
Survival through the art of leaving certain things unsaid.

Sometimes the past returns without permission or a warning,
Springing up in ambush when you least expect the fight.
Some scent, a sound, some laugh becomes a trigger in the morning,
Sometimes in the quiet hours, a threat in the night.
Suffocating in the memories that flood back without end,
Suddenly you're in your teens again, in moments you can't mend.

Some say that time can heal, that it can bring relief,
Space and distance from the pain can make any memory fade.
Still the hurt never lightens, doesn't surrender to that belief,
Settling instead as constant weight, a debt that must be paid.
Sealed away but never gone, does not dissolve or fade to gray,
Simply settles in as a permanent companion that will stay.

So decades later here you stand, still carrying the weight,
Sealed boxes sit in the attic of your mind, in the corners of your soul.
Some secrets are too costly, too dangerous to state,
Some truths must stay locked up to keep you feeling whole.
Survival looks like living with the ghosts nobody sees,
Secrets that you'll carry to your grave, your final mysteries.

VERSE 4

Summer vacation for every kid growing up means freedom – real freedom, the kind you don't truly understand again until much later in life. No alarm clocks jolting you awake at dawn, no 'just 5 more minutes mummy' while yanking the blanket back onto your face, no more homework stealing your evenings, no teachers, no bullies, no performance anxiety crushing your chest.

Just open days and long nights doing whatever brings you peace. Staying up late into the night indulging in your hobbies – gaming, reading, writing, whatever makes you feel alive – knowing you can sleep in tomorrow without consequence.

Maybe there's a family vacation, a trip somewhere that feels like an adventure, or a visit to a relative's place, a break from the familiar reminding you that the world is far bigger than your struggles.

Of course, summer isn't eternal, and eventually the back-to-school ads appear, new supplies are purchased and that familiar knot returns to your stomach.

But for a few golden weeks, you're not counting down the hours to the next day. You're just… free.

SUMMER'S KISS

The final school day ended, it set us free,
We'd run out those doors wild with endless glee,
No alarm clocks, homework, or early dawns to bear,
Just summer stretching endless everywhere.

Those first few mornings felt new every time,
More time for our hobbies, just sublime.
No one to judge us, no obligations at all,
Just freedom answering our every call.

The nights stayed unclaimed by ticking stress,
We owned our time, we were truly blessed.
No guilt for staying up past midnight's chime,
Tomorrow held no rush, we had the time.

Sometimes a journey called us from our door,
A vacation, a trip to places we'd explore.
New sights and sounds that broke monotony,
The world was bigger than we thought it to be.

And if not somewhere new, a relative's embrace,
With grandparents or aunts and uncles we'd stay.
In crowded rooms with lots of noise,
Old photo albums, laughter and borrowed toys.

Even the boredom felt like something sweet,
Long afternoons with nothing to complete.
We'd wander aimlessly or simply sit,
Such a privilege it was, wasn't it?

HOLIDAY MODE...
SCHOOL

Eventually the store windows would change,
Bright signs announcing something more arranged.
School clothes stacked, shoes set by the door,
Summer winding down, time we couldn't restore.

But for a while, before the circle turned again,
Before the days were to be measured and planned,
We tasted joy in every moment's kiss,
Suspended there, and life was just bliss.

VERSE 5

First love rarely announces itself. It doesn't arrive because we were searching for it or ready for it. Often it begins quietly - a friend of a friend, instant chemistry, sparks that feel like destiny.

Suddenly there are secret meetings, held hands, late-night texts and calls that stretch far past reason.

Futures are imagined with certainty, promises are made with absolute conviction, even though neither person truly knows who they are yet or where they're going. When we're young, 'forever' feels not just possible, but probable.

Looking back now with fondness at how consuming it was, how serious every moment felt, how beautiful that naivety was. First love teaches you what it means to be swept away completely.

NEWFOUND SYMPHONY

First love arrives like lightning without warning,
You meet someone new, a glance across a room,
Flowery magic in the air that extraordinary morning,
The chemistry is undeniable, electric, in full bloom,
The sparks feel less like chance and more fate adorning.

That first date in secret carries nervous energy,
Hearts racing faster than they've ever raced before.
Words flow between you with unexpected synergy,
Minutes stretch to hours, yet time flows no more,
Standing still in awe of this newfound symphony.

How can a stranger feel this familiar?
How can conversations last all afternoon?
Each shared laugh makes the connection clearer,
Time bends around this unexpected boon,
Heartbeats syncing to rhythms beautifully peculiar.

Phone screens glow at midnight, then two, then three,
Texts back and forth stretching into dawn.
Sleep's less important than the urgency,
To share one more thought before the moment's gone.
Rivers of romance flowing fluently.

Promises of forever spoken without hesitation,
Plans sketched out for decades yet unlived.
The future seems so clear in youthful imagination,
Every dream together easily believed,
No room for doubt in such complete infatuation.

Only with time does perspective settle in,
Gentle, amusing, the stories now retold.
Not everything imagined could begin,
Not every promise made could truly hold,
Yet the sincerity was real, not false within.

Looking back with fondness at that fire,
How consuming every moment used to feel.
The magnitude of a young heart's desire,
The way young love turned ordinary to surreal,
A flame that couldn't help but inspire.

There's beauty in that blind conviction,
The way forever felt so absolutely real.
That innocent, all-consuming pure addiction,
The intensity of everything we feel,
First love remains our most intense affliction.

It stays with us like gentle waves,
The echoes linger, the wisdom quietly kept.
Not blueprints for how love enslaves,
But a reminder of how fully the heart once leapt,
Before learning how the ground behaves.

VERSE 6

When we're young and through the awkward early teens, friendships are often a numbers game – casting wide nets, hoping something sticks. Some connections work for a while, others fizzle out quickly, and many feel surface-level at best.

But then it happens. You meet people who share your passions, understand the references you make, and more importantly, who like you not despite your quirks but because of them. It's at that moment you recognize: 'These are my people.'

They might be classmates, kids from your neighborhood, maybe one of your cousins, or even coworkers years down the line. The where doesn't matter – what matters is that click, that sense of true belonging. Over time they become more than friends, they become your ride or die family, proving the truth that not all family is bound by blood.

This poem celebrates those chosen bonds that shape who we become.

COMFORT FOOD

Before knowing better, we try everywhere,
Tasting different meals to find what feels right.
Different foods with different faces we share,
Some make us gag, others tastefully delight.
A few lunches work out, a few dinners fall apart,
But rarely a resonance is felt within our heart.

But then we find the dish that feels like home,
That perfect blend of flavors on our tongue.
No more pretending, no more need to roam,
A meal that celebrates the songs we've sung.
No need for condiments or adjusting the spice,
Our comfort food discovered, worth any price.

Can be many dishes too, not limited to one,
From different kitchens and different homes.
Can be from anywhere under the sun,
Found at school, next door, through screens and phones.
The origin doesn't matter, just the shared meal,
What matters is the nourishment we feel.

We cook our buffet with chosen ingredients,
Late nights sharing recipes and tasting dreams.
Inside jokes seasoning our shared experience,
Indulging till we're bursting at the seams.
Our uniqueness savored, we're not wanted bland,
We have help in our kitchen now, lending a mixing hand.

These meals sustain us through our growing years,
The people who savored us and we savored too.
We became each other's comfort, mutual cheers,
Connected by our cravings, pure and true.
They shaped our souls, just as we shaped their outlook,
Each person a recipe in a best-selling cookbook.

This banquet proves that family transcends blood,
Sometimes it's made by those who pull a chair.
Through famine, feast, through bitter and through good,
These are the people worth every meal we share.
Our ride or die, our chosen table spread,
The family we've gathered, souls well-fed.

VERSE 7

The internet gave us something our parents never had growing up – the ability to find kindred spirits anywhere on this rock.

In this digital age, the world has grown smaller, and sometimes your closest friends can be some people you've never physically hugged or sat beside, yet those who know you deeply.

Some of the most genuine connections now form through social media, messaging apps, or online games, connecting people who would have never crossed paths otherwise.

There's something profound about bonds built purely on conversation, on shared thoughts and laughter that transcend physical distance. No coffee shop dates, no sleepovers, yet the connection feels as real as any friendship that began in a classroom, park, bar or a pub.

Sometimes the people who understand you best are the ones you've never met in person, and that doesn't make them any less real or important.

ACROSS DIGITAL OCEANS

I met her where no footsteps tread,
In quiet rooms where words are said.
A glowing screen, a distant name,
Yet something sparked, a gentle flame.

Her words were soft, her wit was bright,
A little sun in endless night.
I'd type, she'd type – the hours flew,
As if in our hearts, each other we already knew.

No gaze to meet, no hand to hold,
Just stories shared, both new and old.
Her laughter lingered on my screen,
A melody, though heard unseen.

We wandered through our worlds and dreams,
Her words like rivers, soft and clean.
I felt her kindness touch my mind,
A rare connection, sweet and blind.

What were the odds, this tiny thread,
Across digital oceans where screens are fed?
Yet somehow there, between the lines,
Her spirit met a part of mine.

So here we are, though worlds apart,
Two strangers sharing open hearts.
A simple chat, yet more it seems,
A friendship born in digital streams.

VERSE 8

Your first breakup doesn't just hurt – it detonates like a nuclear bomb. Is it dramatic? Absolutely. Does it feel catastrophic? Like the sun won't rise tomorrow. Apocalyptic even? Like the world as you've known it has been cancelled forever.

It feels like happiness was a limited resource and you've just been told the supply has run out. You lock yourself in your room, eating ice-cream straight from the tub and listening to playlists that sing exclusively of heartbreak. Every song feels personally targeted.

At that age, there's no perspective, there's no
"You'll get over it" – it IS game over.

Looking back, there's humor in how serious it all felt, how convinced you were that you'd never recover. But in that moment?
It really was the most devastating thing ever.

COURT MARTIAL

I was summoned without warning or appeal,
A message marked urgent, subject line severe.
No explanation, no chance to repeal,
Just a sinking feeling settling in real,
Court was now in session, judgment near.

I stepped inside and froze at what I saw,
The judge was her, the one who used to smile.
She sat there wielding relationship law,
Every tender moment now a fatal flaw,
My partner turned prosecutor at my trial.

The charges were read with procedural grace:
Too clingy at times, too eager to please,
Failure to remember an important date,
Used the wrong emoji to communicate,
And how dare I even talk to another she!

I stammered through objections, tried to fight,
But evidence was stacked impossibly high.
My lawyer (me) had no rebuttal right,
The prosecution's case was airtight,
The verdict determined – guilty was I.

She banged the gavel, heavy, firm and fast,
Dishonorably discharged without delay.
No appeal allowed, the verdict was cast,
My rank stripped bare, belonging to the past,
The romance ending on that day.

My room was my prison in that pure defeat,
Junk foods, my fellow prisoners that night.
Each heartbreak anthem on repeat,
Each song made misery feel complete,
Each lyric slicing with surgical spite.

Returning to civilian life felt strange,
The uniform of 'us' no longer worn.
My routines forced to rearrange,
My familiar world now forced to change,
Relearning how to stand alone.

In time the case became easier to tell,
Filed away under youthful crimes.
Still, for the record, let it be said well:
I loved like it mattered, loved like it fell,
And would probably plead guilty every time.

VERSE 9

Contrary to logic, not all pressure in life is born of failure. Most of it actually comes from expectations.

Education is supposed to be about learning, but somewhere along the way it becomes about scores, ranks and especially comparisons.

Your parents compared you to someone else's kid who got perfect scores. Teachers compared you to last year's students. All too often, this echoes into adult life when your professional milestones are compared to your peers. It becomes a cycle you cannot escape and you quickly learn that your worth comes with terms and conditions.

And the cruelest part? If you've been labeled 'bright' or 'gifted' – the pressure doubles. You're told you're capable of greatness, which means anything less feels like you're wasting your gifts. Meanwhile, every achievement by your peers becomes ammunition. "See what they managed? You could do that too if you tried harder."

The worst part is being stuck between two messages: "You're not good enough" and "You're so talented" – often in the same conversation.

This poem is for anyone who was ever stuck between these two sticky buns and who eventually realized they were more than a percentage on a page.

TREADMILL OF ACHIEVEMENT

They said school was about education and growth,
But somewhere it morphed into a different game.
Where scores became currency, rankings an oath,
And every report card carried your name,
Like a public announcement of success or both,
Your worth and your family's pride or shame.

The comparisons started early, never ceased,
Someone else's kid was always better somehow,
Straight A's, medals, scholarships released,
Like grenades at dinner tables with nary a grin.
"They got this far, so let's speak,
About why you can't seem to win?"

The teachers spoke of the ghosts of last year's class,
The mythical students who never made mistakes,
They set a benchmark you could not surpass,
No matter the effort or concentration it takes.
You're running on a treadmill made of glass,
Watching everyone else through the cracks and breaks.

And if they stamped you with the 'gifted' seal,
Congratulations – now the stakes are higher,
They'll praise your mind and how you think and feel,
Then ask why excellence hasn't caught fire,
Each ordinary outcome they'll appeal,
As proof you're not living up to your entire.

Underachiever
Wasted Potential

Each time a peer succeeded, out came the blade,
"They managed that – why haven't you?
With all your talent, think of what you've made,
Or rather, what you haven't gotten through,"
Every win around you felt like a crusade,
Against the underachiever labeled you.

The math never added up, never made sense,
Told you're talented in the very same breath,
That asked why you weren't better, more intense,
Two messages battling each other to the death,
"You're not good enough" meets "You're immense,"
Both squeezing you until there's nothing left.

The race continues past the graduation stage,
Your job becomes the new report card game,
Promotions, titles, climbing up the wage,
Still measuring yourself against their name,
The script is different but it's the same page,
And worth still comes with footnotes full of shame.

Yet slowly you begin to understand,
You're more than rankings carved into stone,
More than the metrics they had planned,
More than achievements that were never your own,
The race continues, but you can stand,
And realize your worth was always your own.

VERSE 10

The world loves early bloomers. Those prodigies who knew their calling even before hitting their teens, the entrepreneurs who launched before becoming adults, the people who have their lives figured out before they can order a drink.

They speak confidently about five-year plans and ten-year goals while you're still figuring out what you want for lunch.

It's not that you lack ambition - you just lack the certainty that seems to come so naturally to others. And every "What's your plan?" question from relatives, teachers, or friends feels like an accusation.

This poem is for anyone who's tired of pretending they have it figured out, who's learning that late blooming doesn't mean never blooming, and that some of the best journeys don't follow any map at all.

It's about realizing that growth doesn't follow a single timeline, and that not knowing your destination doesn't mean you're lost. Sometimes it just means your path is still forming.

EVERYONE HAS A PLAN (BUT ME)

They had it figured out by age thirteen,
CEOs and doctors, destinies that gleam.
I can't even commit to a coffee routine,
I'm still googling "how to find your dream?"
Everyone has a plan (but me).

At family gatherings the question always lands,
"What's your trajectory looking like?"
I wave my hands and talk of shifting sands,
While some cousin PowerPoints his upward spike.

They speak of five-year plans and goals galore,
Milestones charted like a business degree.
I'm still deciding what streaming service to pay for,
Can't even pick a show to binge-watch weekly.
Everyone has a plan (but me).

Tech bros coded apps at seventeen,
Millionaires before they could keep their alcohol down.
I can't even update my LinkedIn clean,
Or write a bio without an existential breakdown.

Career
Passion
Stability
Money
???

They navigate life like GPS-guided tours,
Every turn calculated, route optimized.
I'm using a crumpled map from outdated stores,
Hoping it hasn't been completely revised.
Everyone has a plan (but me).

"So what's your plan?" they ask with a smile,
Like it's simple, like everyone just knows.
I stumble through answers all the while,
Watching their certainty as mine erodes.

It's not about the drive, I've got that in spades,
Just lacking the compass that points them true.
Their futures are blueprints, mine's still in shades,
A draft that keeps changing its view.
Everyone has a plan (but me).

But late blooming isn't the same as lost,
Just a different map, a longer route.
Some paths take time, and that's the cost,
Of finding one that's genuinely you.

VERSE 11

Turning eighteen was supposed to change everything. I expected people to suddenly see me differently; treat me like I'd crossed some threshold into maturity. Instead, I woke up on my eighteenth birthday feeling exactly like I had at seventeen; just a day older, no wiser, no different.

The world promised this moment would mean something, but in the grand scheme of things, it was just another Saturday. There was no manual, no sudden clarity, no transformation. Just the same person now carrying the label of being an adult that felt both exciting and terrifying, mourning what was left behind while standing at the edge of everything unknown.

Becoming an adult wasn't a single moment of transformation, but a slow accumulation of expectations, freedoms, and consequences; arriving all at once, without instruction, only fully understood in hindsight.

Adulthood wasn't a destination – it was a maelstrom, and I was already spinning in it.

THROUGH THE MAELSTROM

Another year around the sun,
I woke up the same as the day before.
The date had changed, everything else stayed still,
No sudden wisdom waiting at the door.
The mirror showed what it had always shown,
Just older by a day, nothing else had grown,
Yet eighteen felt like stepping into the unknown.

Was I supposed to feel different somehow?
A confidence, a knowing how to stand.
Instead I felt more lost than yesterday,
Yet a familiar stranger in a familiar land.
More questions than before, and no clear plan,
More doors that opened onto disarray,
Excitement and terror walking hand in hand.

The crown of an adult hung above my head,
A weight that I wasn't ready for,
The rules had shifted but nobody said how,
A manual missing from this unread lore,
A change had started though I couldn't see,
Slowly becoming someone undefined,
Caught between who I was and who I would be.

New freedoms came carrying hidden costs,
Choices mattered more than it seemed fair,
The safety nets removed, the training wheels lost,
There were no instructions folded in the air,
No sudden clarity, no master key,
Just more decisions, more to lose or fear,
Choices multiplied but felt less clear.

Adulthood
Childhood

Only with distance does the shape appear,
The way the current gathered speed and sound.
What felt like standing still was movement, clear,
A slow, relentless spinning all around.
Not a beginning marked by solid ground,
Nor an ending meant to finally arrive,
But learning how to stay upright while bound.

So this was adulthood without the fanfare,
Not lightning strike but slow accumulation.
Just navigating the busy thoroughfare,
Learning with each test and tribulation.
No single moment marked where the territory lay,
Just gradual, relentless transformation in sway,
The maelstrom swirls, and there's no other way.

VERSE 12

Lucky are those rare souls whose first love story never needs a sequel. But most of us? That early relationship – the one wrapped in teenage intensity and dramatic promises – it's beautiful but unsustainable. The first real relationship often comes years later, after we've learned the hard lessons.

Maybe it's in college, maybe after we've started working and have figured out where the raindrops fall after we step out from under our parent's umbrella. And this is the relationship where we learn the unglamorous truths: That love languages matter, that our baggage affects how we connect, where affection has to co-exist with misunderstandings, compromises, insecurities, and the weight of two unfinished people trying to grow at the same time.

It's messier, less cinematic, but more honest. We discover that real love means seeing someone's flaws clearly and choosing them anyway - not because we're blind to the problems, but because we're committed to working through them. Whether it lasts or not, this is where we learn that sustainable love is built, not found.

BEYOND THE FAIRY TALE

There are souls who never need a second try,
Their first love story perfect, start to end.
The rest of us? We had to say goodbye,
To teenage dreams too fragile to defend.
That early love was all combustion, heat,
A wildfire beautiful while it burned.
The real thing came when we chanced to meet,
Another person with the wisdom earned.

It showed up after we'd been rained on,
After storms had taught us how to stand.
Early adulthood or further down the road we'd gone,
When we'd learned to walk without a guiding hand.
No longer sheltered by our childhood care,
Rolling in the world's mud, decidedly not neat,
This time we met someone equally stripped bare,
Stumbling, falling, we helped each other to our feet.

This was where we felt the pretty illusions crack,
The butterflies in our stomach still felt nice,
But the youthful passion we had looking back,
Needed lessons in compromise and sacrifice.
We each brought our habits, histories, our fears,
The ways we learned to love, to guard, to cope.
Affection shared space with journeys of past years,
With patterns formed long before this new hope.

There were no grand gestures fit for a screen,
No swelling soundtrack to signal the scene.
Just days stitched together, ordinary, unseen,
And nights where understanding stood in between.
Love showed its shape in the unremarked hours,
In staying to talk when leaving felt fair.
In choosing repair over claiming power,
In learning when to soften, when to care.

We learned to see the flaws without the filter,
The irritating habits, how they shut down or retreat.
And we chose each other, feelings not off-kilter,
By the imperfections we could finally meet.
Real love means seeing someone's broken parts,
And not demanding they be whole or fixed.
Not ignorance but knowledge in our hearts,
That perfection and commitment aren't mixed.

Whether it lasted or quietly ended,
This love left a permanent mark behind.
The knowledge of how connection is tended,
Not found perfect, but patiently designed.
Beyond the fairy tale, in light of reality,
It taught what partnership truly entailed,
Not the vows of magical sensuality,
But the promise to show up even when it paled.

VERSE 13

Your first job search is a special kind of hell. You're supposed to have experience to get experience, which is a paradox nobody bothers explaining. So you sit there, crafting resumes and cover letters with the hope that somebody thinks that you're capable of more than what these pieces of paper convey.

Send. Refresh. Rejection. Repeat.

A thousand applications disappear into the void of online job sites, only to be answered by automated emails thanking you for your interest.

You rehearse fake enthusiasm for companies you researched an hour ago, and question whether or not you chose the right field of work entirely. The questions are absurd too – "Where do you see yourself in five years?" (Who knows? Why not four years? Why not six?) – but you deliver your rehearsed answer with that same manufactured enthusiasm.

Then one day, you get the call. The relief is immense – until you realize this is just the beginning. First day nerves, imposter syndrome, the creeping suspicion you have no idea what you're doing. Adult life has officially begun whether you're ready or not. The job search is a rite of passage nobody adequately prepares you for.

BECAUSE RENT IS DUE

A childhood of lectures, exams and sleepless nights,
They promised opportunities would appear.
Instead you're trapped in qualification fights,
Rose-tinted glasses removed, the real sights,
The journey has begun; destination unclear.

The cursor blinks, you invent a professional past,
"Organizational skills" from getting homework done,
As "Managed a team" are college projects cast,
Somehow making mediocrity sound vast.
Pretending to be a more accomplished person.

Cover letters multiplying as rabbits in spring go,
Company names swapped out, but paragraphs the same.
Writing "passionate about" so much you barely know,
What passion even means in this repetitive show,
Your own story becomes a foreign, manufactured frame.

Click. Submit. The portal swallows whole,
Your carefully crafted exaggeration disappears.
Within the hour, comes back the troll,
Carrying the "Unfortunately," automated scroll,
Another rejection email leers.

"Entry-level position" reads the job ad screen,
"Three years required" when you click the link,
You still get called, but their questions are lean,
The same old "Tell us, why our company?" routine,
"Because, my dear sir, the rent is due," you think.

REJECTION
REJECTION EMAIL
ENTRY

JOB APPLICATIONS

Video interviews mean professional shirt on top,
Pajama bottoms hidden safely out of frame.
You talk till your interviewer has you stop,
Then wait with confidence you haven't got,
While playing this exhausting corporate game.

After countless tries, a company says "You're hired."
Offer letter read on repeat till it feels real.
The celebration lasts until you've perspired,
Then panic strikes – you're actually required,
To show up and pretend you know the deal.

First day nerves and systems you don't understand,
Pretending you're qualified seems ridiculously funny.
Your career has begun but you've got nothing planned,
You'd rather be on a beach full of sand,
But you show up anyway because you need the money.

VERSE 14

Nobody tells you about the secret second half of your job when you get hired. They interview you about skills and experience, but the actual job is 50% work and 50% political theater.

There are unspoken rules nobody explains: the boss's pet gets opportunities regardless of merit and staying late matters more than actual productivity. You finish your tasks efficiently and go home? That's a mark against you. Others scroll social media till two hours past the end of the work day and get praised for "dedication."

The smokers bond over cigarettes and inside jokes, forming an alliance you can't join without destroying your lungs. You don't drink? Good luck bonding at mandatory "optional" happy hours. They say hard work gets rewarded, but really, it's about who laughs at the manager's jokes.

HR insists "we're a family" but families don't make you compete for scraps of approval.

BUT HR SAYS WE'RE A FAMILY

"But HR says we're a family," I said,
As I stood there with my mouth agape,
My manager explained with confidence instead,
A policy that made no logical shape.
I nodded along, conditioned to comply,
While thinking "family" was corporate's favorite lie.

The boss has favorites, that much is clear,
They get the projects while I get the scraps.
My work is solid but I'm not in the sphere,
Of chosen ones who avoid the traps.
Merit doesn't win when you're not celebrated,
But HR really stresses that we're related.

Smokers vanish in groups multiple times a day,
The sacred guilds where decisions are made.
I don't destroy my lungs, so I'm away,
From bonding rituals of the nicotine brigade.
Either wreck your health or watch your chances fade off,
Are these what "family values" are made of?

"Team drinks tonight – it's optional!" they cheer,
Translation: miss it and you're out of the loop.
I mention my real family, they say "Next time, dear,"
But promotions go to the drinking group.
Belonging is earned by poisoning your liver,
Because this family requires a sacrifice forever.

Pizza Party!
PIZZA PARTY
PIZZA
PIZZA
PIZZA
PIZZA
GROAN
GROAN
GROAN
GROAN

They praise those who linger with nothing to do,
Scrolling devotion till well after dark.
Finish early? That reflects poorly on you,
Efficiency lacks the performative spark.
Productivity's fine, but appearances win,
The job's half labor, half learning when to grin.

So here I sit, playing this unspoken game,
Laughing at jokes that aren't remotely funny.
Pretending office politics aren't lame,
While wondering if it's all about the money.
I came here to work, not to master strategy,
But didn't HR say that we're a family?

VERSE 15

You don't realize how much trust matters until someone destroys it completely. When betrayal comes from someone you loved for years, whether a cheating partner, a backstabbing friend or abandoning guardian, anyone you knew (or thought you knew) and who knew you inside out – that wound cuts deeper than heartbreak. It's not just about losing them; it's about losing your ability to believe in anyone at all.

Not all betrayal ends a relationship immediately. Sometimes the person who hurt you is someone you've loved for so long that they're woven into the fabric of your life. Sometimes, you care about your betrayer enough to give them another chance to hurt you. You convince yourself people can change, that love is worth fighting for, that what you had was too precious to abandon. So you forgive, rebuild, try to forget what you know. For a while, it feels right.

Until it happens again. The second betrayal destroys because this time you chose to stay. You handed them the weapon and watched them use it. The person you're angriest at isn't just them – it's yourself.

This poem is about that break in your psyche, and the years it takes to even begin repairing it.

THE LONG SHADOW

We built our world on years of trust and time,
You knew my fears, my dreams, my every climb.
The sword was I and you were my sheathe,
You were the quill, I – the book underneath.
I thought I knew you deeply in your prime,
Until I saw the monster beneath.

The moment truth revealed itself that day,
I watched our world collapse and fall away.
The person standing there wore your face,
But something darker occupied that space.
Everything I trusted turned to gray,
A stranger now stood in your place.

But history doesn't vanish with betrayal's sting,
Love clings to hope like a desperate thing.
You promised change, I wanted to believe,
That forgiveness was something I could achieve.
So I gave another chance, let you back in,
Until the second cut you'd conceive.

The pain became a living, breathing weight,
A constant ache that I could not sedate.
The person I had been before was gone,
Replaced by someone barely holding on.
I drowned in hurt I couldn't articulate,
Living a shadow of the life I thought I'd drawn.

The worst part wasn't crying through the night,
But waking up and having to face the light.
Did you ever love me like you said,
Or was it all a lie inside your head?
I fake-smiled through days, never feeling right,
Wondering if our truth was always dead.

The anger burned at you for what you'd done,
For breaking us when we'd well begun.
But worse, the cannon of fury I aimed at me,
For not noticing the patterns I could clearly see.
I handed you the loaded, smoking gun,
And you fired twice into my corpse with glee.

Trust doesn't break - it shatters into dust,
Fragments too small to ever re-adjust.
You didn't just betray, you also stole that day,
My ability to believe what anyone would say.
Every wall demolished, rebuilt with distrust,
Keeping me trapped within, keeping the world away.

The years that followed stretched impossibly long,
Empty months of keeping everyone gone.
I dissected every word that people said,
Searching for the lies inside my head.
Could I believe someone, did their truth belong?
Or would they leave me broken, cold and dead?

They say that healing comes with passing time,
That one day you'll recover from the crime.
But they don't warn how long you'll be confined,
How many years before you free your mind.
It wasn't months that helped me before I was fine,
Several long years before I left the pain behind.

VERSE 16

Not every day needs to be extraordinary. Most of life isn't made of peaks and valleys - it's the flat stretches in between where we actually live. The ordinary Tuesday where nothing remarkable happens. The Saturday morning routine you've done a hundred times. The evening that ends exactly as expected.

There's something serene about days without drama, without crisis, without needing to rise to some occasion. Just existing in the regular motion of your life –
The same routine at home, the familiar commute, small conversations with the same people that won't be remembered tomorrow. These are the days that don't make it into stories we tell, yet they form the foundation of our very life.

Maybe there's peace in the mundane. Maybe ordinary is underrated. Maybe the days without ups or downs are actually the ones that hold us together.

THE SHAPE OF ORDINARY DAYS

The alarm rings at the hour it always does,
We rise and move, muscle memory kicking in.
Our head stops humming its morning buzz,
As we give our daily cup of coffee a spin.

We move through streets we've memorized without a map,
The metro comes and goes with clockwork precision.
Surrounded by the same commuters in the morning trap,
Known faces, nameless people, in our peripheral vision.

The hours pass in rhythm that requires no thought,
Tasks completed not with passion but with practiced ease.
Lunch at the usual time, conversations lightly fought,
Small talk drifting past like autumn leaves on a breeze.

Evening arrives without announcement or surprise,
As we reach home using familiar streets.
Dinner talks and TV screens, as the daylight dies,
Night arrives singing the same old beats.

There's something peaceful in the predictable design,
A rhythm that demands no heroics or grand feat.
No wars to wage, no impossible hills to climb,
Just the understated blessing of routine complete.

These days won't echo through the years ahead,
Won't become the tales we share when looking back.
Sewing the satchel of our souls, they're the thread,
Stitches that stop our lives from falling slack.

In the script of our lives, they are the binder,
These ordinary days giving us shape as they flow.
Not every moment needs to be a lasting reminder,
Some days can simply come and quietly go.

VERSE 17

The first time death takes someone we love, it feels impossible to survive. But we do. Then it happens again. And again. The grandparent whose hands held generations of stories. The friend who wasn't supposed to leave this early. The parent we thought we'd have more time with. The relative who was our favorite to visit. Each goodbye is different - sudden or expected, peaceful or devastating; they all leave the same permanent ache.

Letting such grief fade from memory is impossible. What fades is the sharpness - the raw, gasping pain. As time moves on, most days we don't even think about it. Other days it crushes us without warning - a song, a smell, an anniversary, and suddenly we're drowning in their absence all over again.

This poem is about the permanence of loss, the way it never truly leaves, just shifts and settles into the architecture of who we become.

FISHERMAN OF GRIEF

The reaper introduced itself without a sound,
Left an absence where happiness used to be.
The silence was the loudest thing around,
A void that stretched as far as we could see,
The dead can't listen to the cries of those yet living free.

The heavens don't stop at claiming one,
Angels came for grandparents; in their laps we played.
They took the friends whose lives had just begun,
Leaving behind memories, raw and flayed.
Each absence carved a wound that wouldn't heal,
Left it scratched, sliced, burned till we couldn't feel.

We start to wonder if we said enough,
Did they know how much they truly meant?
The final conversations, were they too rough?
The visits we postponed, the time not spent,
Regret becomes a pill, bitter and tough,
The words unsaid, the love we never sent,
We choke swallowing it, without a cough.

They swore that grief would fade with time,
Eventually the pain would go away.
The sharpness dulls, it's true, no longer prime,
But the loss still haunts some odd quiet day,
That hollow space where loved ones used to play.

Most mornings, years later, forget the heavy ache,
New memories helping the old ones to move on.
But some familiar hook catches, and we forsake,
All composure, pulled back to what's now gone.
We're pulled to the boat of memories, can't break away,
The fisherman of grief slowly reels in his prey.

Some days mark themselves in permanent ink,
Birthdays they'll never see, dates carved in stone.
We keep their contact saved, their social media's link,
Even call their number, to just hear the tone.
Far in the distance, their memories still wink,
Reminding us that we're not alone,
That they still live in bonds that will never shrink.

We learn to live with these ghosts in our chest,
Not haunting us but keeping us aware.
That love doesn't go away when they eternally rest,
It just becomes part of our daily prayer.
We honor them by living at our best,
Loving others as they love us, even knowing of the snare,
That one day we too, will hug Death's breast.

VERSE 18

My own mind was supposed to be a safe space, but it happened... it turned hostile against me. The voice inside my head became a constant stream of criticism, telling me that I was too much and not enough at the same time, that I never belonged anywhere, and I never would. I felt like a burden, I thought that everyone would be better off without me, that there was no point in trying anything because I'd fail anyway.

People asked me, "What's wrong?" and I replied, "Nothing," because how could I explain that I was trapped inside my own head, watching myself sabotage my every move while feeling powerless to intervene.

The guilt compounded the pain: "I should be grateful. Others have it worse. What's wrong with me?" I was drowning in plain sight and no one could see it.

Mental health struggles are often battles fought in the isolation of your own mind. This poem is for anyone who's ever battled their own thoughts, who's felt broken while looking whole, who's wondered if they'll ever feel like themselves again.

INVISIBLE WAR

They invaded my land, ransacked my court,
Infiltrated every corner of my mental fort.
Bad thoughts in my head, where I was once whole,
Echo soldiers with voices beyond control.
They burned my farms with insecurities and doubts,
Growing stronger while hollowing my kingdom out.

They whispered poison through my castle walls,
"You're worthless, you're a burden, you'll always fall."
"You were never supposed to be the king,"
Each morning did their propaganda sing.
My own citizens made their will brutally clear,
"You don't belong; you were never wanted here."

Ones still loyal asked "My lord, are you distressed?"
"Nothing, all is well," I lied, barely holding the crest.
My own court meanwhile sabotaged my reign,
While I was powerless to stop my kingdom's pain.
I admit that I'd become a puppet monarch in play,
While darker forces pulled my strings each day.

The voices turned my guilt into a sword,
"Other kingdoms suffer far worse than yours."
"You're just pathetic, weak beyond belief."
"You have no right to feel this kind of grief."
They convinced me that I was unworthy of the crown,
That everyone would cheer if I were to step down.

Some days I rallied an army to defend,
Each moment conquered bringing relief profound.
But every time, again, I had to bend,
As more enemy forces circled me around.
The battlefields of this war, none could perceive,
No wounds to show that I was dying, make people believe.

I accused the universe for turning on me,
Blamed destiny for attacking from air, land and sea.
Asked why misery found my castle gates easily,
What angered gods to make this their decree?
The royal palace being dismantled stone by stone,
Conquest nearing each sunrise as I was weaker and alone.

It didn't feel like peace would ever find my land again,
Never felt like I could go back to before it all began.
Forever trapped inside this living hell,
I banged on the walls of my mental shell.
The fight continued with no dawn in sight,
I still drowned in blood, and died each night.

VERSE 19

There's a specific kind of loneliness that comes from craving connection we so often can't find. Not friendship, but real love. We think of our perfect soulmate and imagine what they would look and sound like - someone we haven't met yet (or maybe never will), and our heart aches day and night for something that doesn't exist yet.

It often feels like traversing a dark cityscape with a power outage. All we want is someone to hold our hand and say, "Let's figure this out together." But the stranger we dream of remains just that - a stranger. Maybe real, maybe imagined.

This poem is about that relentless search for love, and the fear that we might run out of time to find it.

STRANDED

I don't know my way in this world,
I haven't yet found my destination.
All I want in this life is some love,
All I've ever wanted is some affection.

I don't know what path to travel,
To find love and devotion waiting for me.
All I want is something real,
Not hollow words or false sympathy.

A stranger's face in my mind's eye,
Haunts me through day and night.
I search for them in every crowd,
Don't know if they're even real or right.

My mind stays fully intoxicated,
I've lost my senses to the silence,
Roaming from thought to thought,
Sometimes peace, sometimes violence.

I don't know my way in this world,
I wish I had a guide to my destination,
I'm tired of waiting for even a sliver of love,
All my mind knows now is crippling frustration.

I wish someone would hold my hand,
Together we could find our destiny,
Get whisked away like leaves in a storm,
The wind saving us both from this monotony.

But alas, I feel I've searched for far too long,
Feels like I'm stranded on this beach.
Life is like footprints in the sand,
And the tide keeps coming in, just out of reach.

VERSE 20

There's a specific moment – we can't always predict when it happens, but we know when it engulfs us. And it's the first time we stop negotiating with our own collapse.

It's never about suddenly being healed or fixed. It's about taking that first step forward and drawing a line in the sand. It's when we stop wallowing in self-pity and tell ourselves, "I'm still here. I'm still wounded. But I'm done asking permission to exist." We've been through hell already – what more can the world possibly do to us?

This poem is about that first moment of rebellion, when we plant our feet and refuse to be pushed back by our demons anymore: Not on that day. Not ever again.

WE'RE BREAKING OUT OF HELL

Demons arrive in forms that cannot be predicted,
Each person carries their own shadow cast.
For me they were voices that heavily restricted,
Moving on from the hellscape of my past.
They wore crowns of smoke, their claws inflicted,
Big weeping gashes, leaving me aghast.
These creatures hunted me, leaving my soul afflicted,
With terror unending, their grips holding fast.

I fell asleep and woke in hell's domain,
On hands and knees in dirt, my face was sliced.
Above me loomed my demons, born of pain,
They laughed and mocked, "Look how you've sacrificed.
Everything good you have, you don't deserve again,
Where did you get off thinking you'd sufficed?"

They asked me, "Did you think you'd ever make it out?
The nerve of you, believing you could survive."
But here's the truth that silenced their shout:
I'd been in hell for years, and I was still alive.
No more did my scars fill my heart with doubt,
Proof I was stronger than what my evils could contrive.
Each wound told stories of the wars I'd fought,
Not weaknesses anymore, but lessons hell had taught.

EXIT

Their whips came down to break me one more time,
But this time my hands caught them mid-descent.
I rose up from the scorching dirt and grime,
Tore off their heads; a crime I didn't repent.
Let their blood flow free like a fiery brine,
I was done with asking what their torture meant.

I turned to face my voices still trapped inside,
The thoughts that cowered in their prison cells.
"Listen to me - no more will we hide,
We've survived the worst that's offered by these dwells.
We're warriors now, battle-scarred with pride,
So gather close, hear what your general tells:
We've bled enough, we've suffered through this spell,
My brothers, sisters - we're breaking out of hell."

VERSE 21

Falling in love is easy. The hard part is getting back up after it ends. We're not afraid of the feeling itself, but of what will come if we have our heart broken again. That feeling of the organ itself pumping blood through our veins, but the heartbeat missing as we realize that we're alone again is one of the worst things a person can feel.

We've seen others make it look effortless, but for some of us, love feels like a series of beautiful disasters. And yet, somehow, we have to find the strength to risk it all over again, knowing full well how it might end.

This poem is about the courage to fall in love repeatedly, even when the broken pieces of our heart are barely held together with tape and super-glue.

GLASS HEART

I'm not afraid to fall in love once more,
To open myself up and let feelings bloom,
I fear what waits on the other side of the door,
Like many who are scared of dying in a lonely room.

I've seen others fall in true love's embrace,
Supporting each other when moments define,
But I've never known love in that sacred space,
Only heard the stories, never called it mine.

I've witnessed love's caring touch unfold,
Heard that it's patient, gentle, kind,
Been told these truths a thousand times,
But that love's a language I've never signed.

I used to dream of grand romantic scenes,
Flowers in hand, a heartfelt sign to hold,
A speech professing what my love means,
And watching our perfect story unfold.

But that never happens, does it now?
No one seems to stick around me for long,
My breaking heart writes these verses somehow,
They keep telling me that life isn't a beautiful song.

As I write these words and bare my soul,
Giving broken thoughts their written form,
Drowning my pupils, losing all control,
Flooded by my mind's emotional storm.

I know that I'll fall in love once more,
Risk this heart made of glass shattering to sand,
If I land on the flip-side of disaster's door,
Here's hoping I find the will to once more stand.

VERSE 22

Remember 2020? The year the world stopped spinning and we all became shut-ins? What started as "just two weeks to flatten the curve" turned into months of increasingly bizarre behavior. We stockpiled toilet paper like it was currency, attended work or school meetings in our pajama bottoms, lost all concept of time – was it Friday? June? Did it even matter anymore?

The rules kept changing, the goalposts kept moving, and somehow, we convinced ourselves we'd emerge from quarantine as productive, enlightened versions of ourselves – finally fluent in a new language, physically fit, creatively fulfilled. Instead, we mostly just survived, developed questionable hygiene habits, and formed parasocial relationships with whatever characters inhabited the shows we binged.

This poem reimagines those surreal months as if we were all trapped inside the world's worst challenge – complete with impossible objectives, confusing instructions, and the difficulty accidentally cranked up to maximum. If you survived lockdown, you earned this laugh.

THE DIFFICULT GAME

The game began in March with our normal lives intact,
But we each picked a character, as our world was attacked.
Some chose "productive home chef" with ambitions so grand,
Others selected "sweatpants hermit" - the most popular brand.

The tutorial said "two weeks" to beat this level's test,
We stocked up on potions and swore to try our very best.
"We'll level up our skills & stats, read the manuals on the shelves!"
Narrator: They did none of those things & forgot to wash themselves.

Just when we thought we'd figured out the game's cruel story,
New Variants appeared like bosses; all was not hunky-dory.
Delta hit us hard, then Omicron came jetting,
The difficulty slider broke - stuck on the "Ultra Hard" setting.

We gathered all the loot we could from every single store,
Toilet paper filled our inventory, then we went back for more.
Hand sanitizer became gold, dry pasta our precious prize,
We built our survival stashes to impossible size.

Some characters seemed to spawn, with faulty AI code,
Some players started acting like they were using a cheat-mode.
"Masks are useless items!" they'd scream at merchants wearing vests,
While the rest of us were trying to run weekly shopping quests.

Time became a broken feature, dates no longer tracked,
Our daily logs bugged, all routines were hacked.
We attended clan meetings with just underwear equipped,
Below the screen was chaos that the webcam kindly skipped.

Class: Pro Snack Eater
Skills: Gluttony
Greed
Chubbiness

We started optional missions with intentions pure and bright,
"I'll learn a new language or to cook," we swore with all our might.
Those quests stayed uncompleted in our logs, forever gray,
While binge-watching shows and snacking filled our actual day.

We'd pause between the levels to get our systems checked,
Two lines meant infection - our progress got wrecked.
One line was like respawning at a checkpoint saved,
Until the next exposure and back to isolation we caved.

The vaccine finally dropped like a boss weapon rare,
But claiming it meant crashing servers everywhere.
We refreshed our browsers a thousand times or more,
Fighting bots and glitches in this pharmaceutical war.

They shut down the servers and said, "The game is finally done!"
But our social skills had died, we'd forgotten 'how to human',
Small talk felt like foreign language, crowds induced our fear,
We'd survived the difficult game, but paid a cost severe.

VERSE 23

There's a specific kind of self-betrayal that comes with hating your body but lacking the will to change it. We know exactly what needs to happen – we need to eat better, move more, stop making excuses.
The roadmap is clear. The execution? Non-existent.

Every morning starts with resolve. Every night ends in disappointment. The mirror becomes an adversary, old photos a painful reminder of who we used to be. The gym membership gathers dust. The clothes in our closet mock us. And somehow, despite hating what we see, we still can't find the motivation to do anything about it.

This poem is about that exhausting disconnect between knowing and doing, between wanting to change and choosing comfort instead, between self-awareness and self-sabotage.

EXERCISE OR EXTRA FRIES

The mirror stares back at me like I owe it rent,
"I swear I'll pay this time," I say, we're both tired of the lies.
It shows me every promise that I swore but never meant,
I swear again I'll change this time, but then I order some fries.

My closet's full of jeans that fit a person from my past,
I keep them like a museum of the body I let go.
"Sizes I'll wear again," but they stay gathering dust,
Instead I wear sweatpants daily, no need to adjust.

My abs exist somewhere beneath the layers I've acquired,
Like buried treasure waiting for an excavation crew.
The fitness that I once had has apparently expired,
Now catching breath from standing is the exercise I do.

Each morning starts heroic, a bottle of optimism I fill,
"Today's the day," I say, like I've said so many times before,
By evening I'm negotiating terms with my will,
Compromise tastes salty, comes in portions for four.

Old photos of me surface, like they're sent to attack,
A version of me who could fit in a two sizes small shirt,
I scroll away and I wince and I promise I'll be back,
Then reward my discomfort with an ice-cream sundae dessert.

I know the formula by heart: burn more than you consume,
Move your body, track your meals, it's simple mathematics.
But knowledge doesn't equal action when you're scrolling in your room,
Eating things you'll regret while watching food-related graphics.

I promise I'll come tomorrow
GYM

Before I sleep, I promise that tomorrow I'll try harder,
I'll be the version of myself that actually follows through.
But morning me and evening me maintain a different charter,
And night returns to find I've disappointed me anew.

I'm laughing, but really crying inside at patterns that I trace,
Fully informed, deeply stuck, self-aware to the brow,
Torn between the treadmills and grease-stained grace,
While hating this body I stubbornly refuse to outgrow.

So here I stand, another day, same question on my plate,
Will today be different or will I continue this pain?
I know the answer I choose is wrong, with myself I'll be irate,
Exercise or extra fries? I'll take the fries again.

VERSE 24

So many times I feel that I'm in the room, but no one acknowledges me. I speak, but my words dissolve into silence. I exist, but barely, like a shadow that everyone walks through without noticing. Many times, I start to believe what their indifference tells me:
I don't belong here. I never did.

The world is full of people who feel like ghosts - present but unseen, breathing but forgotten. Each day is another confirmation that we're temporary, disposable, already halfway gone. The worst part is thinking that when we finally vanish completely, no one will remember we were here at all.

I write this poem to put our struggles with self-worth and what we go through every day into words that, hopefully, the world can understand.

To anyone who's ever felt like they're fading while everyone else stays solid and real, to anyone who has ever felt like an unwanted ghost: I see you, I love you, and I'm here to tell you: You should love yourself too.

GHOST IN THE CROWD

Unwanted... Unneeded... Just another ghost in the crowd,
Unseen... Unnoticed... Vanishing into the mists like a cloud.
A raft of hollowed feelings like rotten driftwood,
Floating in a river of silence beneath a darkening shroud,
Carrying burdens too heavy, every wave threatening to capsize,
One day that raft will sink, swallowed by silence that's too loud.

Unwanted... Unneeded... A silent echo in the mountains,
Unseen... Unnoticed... Just another shadow fading out.
An empty soul floating through the trees,
A presence unnoticed, a heart left unwound.
The slowing heartbeats heard among the cold, restless winds,
One day that soul will vanish, lost without a sound.

Unwanted... Unneeded... like the ash left behind after a fire,
Unseen... Unnoticed... embers cooling in a forgotten mire.
A dying spark that once burned with a blazing roar,
A fading ghost of warmth, soon lost forevermore,
Drifting away on the winds of a desert so dark and old,
One day that ghost of warmth will become a spirit of cold.

Unwanted... Unneeded... like a cracked mural of clay,
Unseen... Unnoticed... fading further each day.
A relic on the walls of a cold, dark spire,
Vanishing from time, an object of no one's desire.
Buried in shadows where forgotten things lay,
One day that relic will simply crumble away.

A spectre fading through alleys of dusk, silence swallowing sound,
Running through teeming streets, yet barren all around.
Breath like a lantern dimmed, its fever finally drowned,
Footprints dissolving in rain, a trace nowhere to be found.
Unseen... Unnoticed... Vanishing into the mists like a cloud,
Unwanted... Unneeded... Just another ghost in the crowd.

VERSE 25

Sometimes our own strength isn't enough. Sometimes the voices in our head are too loud, too harsh, too convincing of the fact that we're not worth saving. On those days, it's not willpower that keeps us afloat – it's the people who refuse to let us sink.

I'm talking about those specific kinds of friends who don't wait for us to ask for help – they just show up. They see the cracks before we crumble. They reach out when we've gone silent. They refuse to accept "I'm fine" when they know it's a lie.

Distance doesn't stop them. Time zones don't matter. Whether they're people we interact with in the physical space or people we've met online in a game or on social media doesn't matter.

What does matter is that phone call that lasts hours, a care package that arrives when you need it most, messages that say "I'm thinking of you" on days you feel forgotten.

This poem is for all those friends who are someone's safety net, who love their people through their "I'm unlovable" moments, who tell their friends every day, with their actions rather than words: "I'm the sunshine, which means that you don't have to face the darkness alone."

THE CRACKED SHELL

An egg with lots of cracks, thin fractures splitting the white,
I felt the shell collapsing, too much pressure from inside.
The weight of what I carried pressing out too hard,
Each new dreadful day left me further cracked and scarred.
The snakes circled me and hissed, they wanted my soul,
This broken egg, too damaged for even them to swallow whole.

But then the hands arrived, gentle warmth against my shell,
They didn't try to hatch me early or cast some magic spell.
Picked me from the ground, to prevent me getting attacked,
Kept my whites and yolk inside, an ability that I lacked.
"Eggs need time and care," they said, and I could clearly tell,
They'd sit beside me, holding me tight as the darkness fell.

Some hands were far away, still crossed the deep divide,
Screens connecting them to me, staying digitally by my side.
The chats were a safe nest, words keeping fear at bay,
Messages that said "You matter" on my most forgotten day.
Some even sent warm gifts, by international post,
Proof that distance couldn't stop their love from coast to coast.

They didn't believe me when I insisted that I was doing well,
Saw the cracks widening, could read the signs and tell.
"You're not fine," they'd say with love, no judgment in their tone,
"We're here to help you through this, you don't have to be alone."
They didn't need me to be perfect or to have it all together,
Just needed me to know they'd hold my shell through any weather.

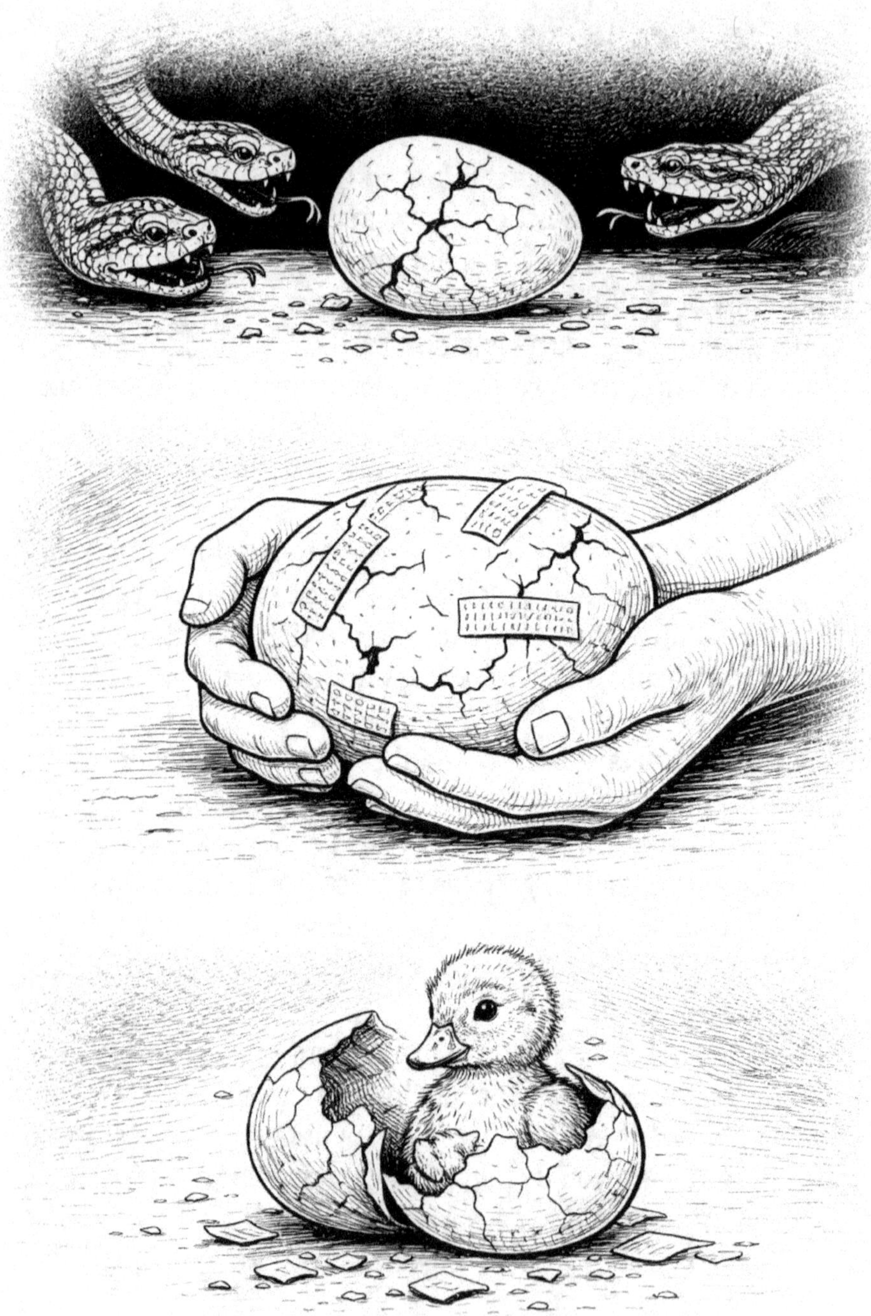

They noticed all the little things I would quietly abort,
Nourished me with their presence, a warmth of support.
Reminded me to shower, sleep, to eat something every day,
The basic tasks I'd forgotten due to my shell's decay.
Became the heating lamp, when from the sky, the sun detached,
Guarding who I used to be until my egg had hatched.

They wrapped me up in tape, used some glue made of care,
Didn't let a single piece break off my fragile layer.
When I was fully certain that I would shatter into dust,
Their love became my incubator, the foundation of my trust.
I borrowed hope from them, when mine had slipped away,
It helped me through so many nights, until I saw the day.

And here's the truth about an egg with cracks along its side:
It doesn't mean the life it carries has withered up and died.
What felt like fatal damage was the beginning of my birth,
The breaking that I feared was proving what my life was worth.
They knew before I knew it that I'd make it through intact,
That cracked and taped-together shells still have a chance to hatch.

They let the shell open in time, when they had a positive inkling,
And out stumbled a wobbly, fuzzy, adorable duckling.
The tape and glue fell away as new life pushed on through,
My friends had kept me whole enough to start again brand new.
They taught me cracked and broken eggs can still emerge as whole,
That friendship is the sunshine that can save a struggling soul.

VERSE 26

Learning to be alone with nothing to keep you company but your thoughts is a very important skill. What it isn't is some "Instagram-worthy" self-love journey with perfect lighting and motivational quotes.

Somewhere between the slight defensiveness you feel when ordering "Just one plate" at a restaurant and the realization that you've been talking to yourself for twenty minutes while cooking at home, the solitude stops feeling like failure and starts feeling like freedom.

You become fluent in your own company. Not because you've given up on love, but because you've stopped waiting for someone else to validate your existence.

This poem is about learning that alone doesn't always mean lonely, and that being good company for yourself might be the best relationship you'll ever have.

<u>NOT A SEQUEL</u>

"Are you still watching?" Netflix asks like it's concerned,
"Yes, next episode," is the answer, I've watched six of them straight.
My couch has a permanent dent to which I always return,
My growing list of shows mocks me, I've got no Friday date.

I tell my houseplants everything, they don't complain at my yapping,
They've become my therapists and I know that sounds absurd,
Even judge me once or twice, I swear, as I water their roots,
But at least they listen better than people, hanging on to every word.

My coffee pot gets a "good morning" and the toaster a high-five,
The mouse of my computer waves the pointer in greeting,
As I check my social media or dive into a single player game,
And equip fancy weapons to give the enemy AI a beating.

I cook a three-course dinner for no one else but me,
Plating food like I'm on some competitive cooking show.
"The presentation's perfect," I announce when I'm done,
Eating it on the couch, watching some old movie that I know.

Then in this repeating routine, something shifted in the air,
The silence stopped accusing me of being somehow incomplete.
My yearning for another shifted into something I could bear.
I realized that my own company is actually pretty sweet.

I perfected my solo script, became a one-person cast,
Not half a story waiting for its ending to be known,
I became a completed work, a masterfully crafted show,
Not the sequel of a movie, but one that stands on its own.

I've learned that fun doesn't require an audience or a crowd,
Sometimes it's really fun to wander solo without a plan.
Dancing in the rain, singing off-key concerts in the street,
Just me and my decisions, living life the best I can.

I'm not swearing off romance or shutting down my heart,
Still hoping that someone special might eventually come over.
I'll keep having fun with my life, my hobbies an Amazonian jungle,
And when they are ready, they can be my explorer.

There's such freedom in needing no one else to be okay,
In building a full life, becoming your own best friend.
Not asking for permission to enjoy your daily life,
Not settling for loneliness, just choosing to transcend.

So cheers to having amazing times alone, to flying free solo,
To learning I'm the main character, not someone's plus-one to be,
To not be half of something missing, I'm already fully grown,
To realizing that sometimes, all I need is the company of me.

VERSE 27

We contain multitudes. The part of us that sees beauty in chaos. The part that wrestles with darkness. The part that holds onto hope even when it seems impossible. Each one has something to teach us; each one helps us navigate a different terrain of being human.

This poem is about the internal journey we all take - through joy and sorrow, doubt and belief, fear and courage.

It's about learning that we're never truly alone, even in our loneliest moments, because we carry within us everything we need to make it through our hardest struggles.

VOICES IN MY MIND

In the liveliest corners of my mind,
A council forms, opinions entwined.
"Guys," I say, like there's a crowd,
These thoughts of mine, both soft and loud.

One argues logic while another just dreams,
Together they sort through my mental extremes.
When I'm alone, they become my voice,
A messy chorus, but still my choice.

They show me laughter mixed with doubt,
Help me figure my chaos out.
So "Guys," I say, while I pace my room,
At least in my head, I'm not alone with the gloom.

In the shadowed corners of my mind,
A silent council, hard to find.
"Guys," I say, to the empty air,
Voices echo, but no one's there.

One whispers sorrow, another despair,
Together they linger, a heavy layer.
In solitude's grip, I wrestle with fears,
A chorus of shadows, a symphony of tears.

Through all my past losses they parade,
Each memory sharp as a razor blade.
So, "Guys," I say, as the darkness creeps near,
In the depths of my thoughts, I'm wrapped in fear.

In the quiet corners of my mind,
A hopeful council, warm and kind.
"Guys," I say, as I breathe in deep,
Voices of courage, in dreams they leap.

One cracks a joke, another shares belief,
Together they weave a comfortable blanket of relief.
In solitude's embrace, I find my light,
A chorus of dreams that shine through the night.

Through challenges faced, they lift me high,
With every whisper, I learn to fly.
So, "Guys," I say, as I rise and strive,
Through shadows and dreams, I learn to thrive.
In the depths of my thoughts, I'm never alone,
A hopeful chorus, leading me home.

VERSE 28

Remember when growing up, the adults told you,
"You'll understand when you get older," and now that
you're older, you're still scratching your head wondering
what they were waffling about?

Were they lying? Did they too gain responsibilities while
feeling like confused teenagers who've somehow gained
access to credit cards and legal documents?
Did they too eventually realize that adulthood isn't a
destination you arrive at – it's a performance you're
constantly rehearsing without ever quite nailing the role?

What follows below is the honest survival guide they
should've given us – the acknowledgment that most of us
are winging it, improvising, and googling basic things we
should probably already know.

Welcome to adulthood: where the answers are made up
and the instructions don't matter.

ADULTING (FOR DUMMIES)

I Googled "slightly tired" and discovered I'm already deceased,
Fourteen tabs of symptoms open, my anxiety's increased.
Doctor's number is in my phone, I could call him if I choose,
But setting up an appointment's scary, I'd rather just refuse.
"I'll go next month," I promise, like I've done for many years,
While the internet convinces me to validate my fears.

This capitalist society says I'll work till I'm burned,
My bosses will build three houses with money that I've earned.
Meanwhile I write monthly budgets I know I won't obey,
That fancy TV, that computer upgrade, through my nose I'll pay.
My balance goes from "comfortable" to "crisis" in a blink,
Netflix, Spotify, and six more apps, subscriptions I forgot to unlink.

Professional email starts with "I hope this finds you well,"
What I'd actually say in person is "Yo, this situation is hell."
My phone changed my signature from "regards" to "regret,"
Autocorrect is my "enema", it truly fills me with dread.
Accidentally told a client "I love you, bye!" while disconnecting a call,
My brain defaulted to family mode, I really dropped the ball.

I searched 'How long to microwave water,' at age thirty-two,
My wardrobe has labels: either 'dirty' or 'if it doesn't smell, it'll do'.
At thirty-five, I still need tutorials on 'How to wear a tie,'
So many things, an adult should know, I don't – I won't lie.
I look up important things, like taxes, to see if I'm on the right track,
But the information I get sends me for a loop, I land flat on my back.

?
?
?
?
BILLS!
MEAL PLANS
REAL PLANS
TAXES
BUY DETERGENT
Adulting
FOR
DUMMIES

"Oh god! Please, no!" I think as a party invitation appears,
I'd rather sit with a book in bed, than socialize with my peers.
Sometimes my social battery definitely needs a good recharge,
I cough into the phone, lying about an infection being at large.
I'll promise "Maybe next time!" with sincerity that's faked,
While silently celebrating plans I've successfully unmade.

Family dinners are akin to a performance on a stage,
"My life is going great!" I say, while I'm trapped in a cage,
I nod at office jargon that I've never really understood,
Pretending I'm a professional and doing what I should.
"My day is going well!" I post on social media feeds,
While living off of takeout and ignoring all my needs.

I've consulted other adults, asked "Please tell me what to do,"
They said with a chuckle, "We're improvising, just as lost as you."
Some seem to have their life together, but it's an elaborate disguise,
Most of us make it up as we go, that's the real funny surprise.
"When do I really start feeling like an adult?" I finally say,
Maybe never, maybe that's okay – we're learning every day.

Step one of growing up was accepting I was underprepared,
It's not that no one taught me anything, what they knew, they shared.
The reality is they too, were just as confused when it was their time.
It's the wheel of life, turning for years, without reason or rhyme.
Would be handy if we had a book while still inside our mummies,
Clearly labeled, a self-help guide: 'Adulting (For Dummies)'

VERSE 29

If you could sit across from your childhood self, what would you say? Would you warn the younger you of all the trials they are yet to overcome? Or would you realize that those struggles are why you're sitting here now, the strongest you've ever been? That you can't spare them the pain without erasing yourself.

This poem is about making peace with that choice, about realizing our younger self didn't need warnings –
They needed to walk through fire to discover they were fireproof. It's a love letter backward through time, saying: "I wish I could spare you, but I'm grateful I can't – because this way, you'll learn that you were always strong enough."

IF I COULD SEND A LETTER

If I could send a letter to the younger, gentler me I used to know,
I'd speak about the innocence that made them pure and bright.
I'd praise them for the kindness to every soul they would show,
Before it was taken by demons that tried to keep me down through the night.
I'd tell them that their softness wasn't weakness, even though,
The world ahead would test them, make them question wrong from right.
I wish I could preserve that version of me, keep it safe from harm,
But growth requires the wintery cold, before we can learn to stay warm.

I remember the path ahead of them, the struggles yet to come,
The times when they'll feel hollow, when the hurt becomes too real.
The days when being seen by others leaves them feeling numb,
When closeness with another seems impossible to feel.
When their heart beats unevenly, like a broken drum,
When despair leaks from the letter they'll get, with a broken seal.
I wish I could absorb it all, protect them from the cost,
But finding who we are requires seasons when we're lost.

Some people will betray them, leave them shattered on the ground,
The kind of wounds that burrow deep and make them doubt it all.
They'll discover that not everyone who's loved will stick around,
That those they held most dear might be the ones who cause their fall.
But something precious hides within each painful, crying sound,
The scars will build their character, make empathy their call.
The cracks that shatter everything will let the healing in,
They'll see that falling down is often where we learn to win.

I want to tell them every storm that's headed for their shore,
To give them maps and warnings, show them how to stay afloat.
But here's the truth I've learned that matters so much more:
They're building something stronger with each painful chapter wrote.
The person they'll become is forged within that inner war,
The strength, the grace, the wisdom - earned, not learned by rote.
If I erased their struggles, I'd erase who they will be,
I can't steal their hard-won victory, even to set them free.

So here's what I would tell them as they face what lies ahead:
They're braver than they believe, more unbreakable than they know.
In the mornings when they're certain that they'd rather stay in bed,
When hope becomes a dying candle, flame barely there to show –
They'll find a way to rise again, to lift their weary head,
Learn to breathe underwater when the waves try to drag them low.
Each time they think they're broken, the collapse becomes their start,
The lava won't destroy them - it will only forge their heart.

One day they'll look back at this moment with grateful tears,
Not because the journey wasn't hard or didn't leave its mark,
But because they walked through the inferno, conquering their fears,
Because they learned to be their own light even in the darkest dark.
They'll understand that all the pain across their worst years,
Was building them into someone who could hold a bigger spark.
So my younger me, you don't need me to be your seer,
You're stronger than you know, and one day, you'll be standing right here.

VERSE 30

This next poem tells the tale of a kid who didn't quite fit in anywhere while growing up, but here's the thing, I suspect parts of it might be your story too.

Far too often does it feel like the world is a giant jig-saw puzzle and you're the wrong-shaped piece. We all have our own versions of the same battles. Different demons wearing different faces, but the same war underneath. Some of us were the bullied kid, the heartbroken romantic, the overlooked employee, the misunderstood soul - all of these things or none of these, fighting another battle entirely. But it's those battles that make us stronger.

This is the story of a fat, chubby kid born in 1990 who grew into an adult and is still trying to figure it all out. Who's realized that his struggles aren't disqualifying him from happiness – they are preparing him for it. I write this ballad to try and put into words what so many of us live through.

Because my story might wear my name, but the truth it tells belongs to all of us.

FROM DARKNESS TO DAWN

Listen to me closely, I'll tell you a story true enough,
About a little 90s kid, we'll call him Baby Fluff,
He was born a little chubby, had a little bit too much hair,
When his mom first saw him, she thought she'd birthed a bear,
As he grew up into a little kid, he was really cute,
But as all kids are, he was unprepared for what life would at him shoot.

Trouble started young for Baby Fluff, the cracks began to show,
The other kids made friends quick, but Baby Fluff was slow.
He wasn't good at outdoor sports, didn't know how to fit in a crowd,
His laughter drowned by cooler kids who were always much too loud,
The bullies found their target, made him wish he could just disappear,
Each day was a battlefield, hiding inside himself was the only frontier.

He found his escape in stories, worlds beyond his reach,
Books with heroes teaching courage that others couldn't teach,
Games where he could be Baby Fluff the brave, the strong, the understood,
Movies showing him that outcasts could turn out to be good,
These fictional companions never judged him, never left,
When reality felt crushing, fantasy stopped him feeling bereft.

Words became his weapons when his body couldn't fight,
He'd write his pain on notebook pages, hidden from the light,
Stories, poems, scattered thoughts - a refuge in the ink,
When people felt too dangerous, he'd let his feelings sink,
Into verses that nobody read, confessions no one heard,
His verses became the only friend who understood his every word.

Over time some friends appeared, a handful who could see,
Past the awkward, past the quiet, found who Baby Fluff could really be,
But social etiquettes and grace eluded him, small talk felt like a test,
He'd rehearse conversations, never quite knowing what to say best,
Even with the ones who cared, he felt like an impostor there,
Playing "normal" was exhausting, like breathing underwater air.

The years rolled by relentlessly, and childhood slipped away,
Adulthood arrived with bills to pay and rent due every day,
He found himself in office chairs, in jobs that paid but didn't fill,
Working just to keep surviving, bending to the corporate will,
The dreams he had of making art replaced by spreadsheets and reports,
Baby Fluff became a worker, creativity on trial in corporate courts.

Then love came crashing through his door like lightning splits the sky,
He gave his heart completely, thought he'd finally learned to fly,
For a while the world was golden, every color shining bright,
She made him feel like maybe he was worthy of the light,
But fairy tales don't last forever, especially for ones like him,
That vixen broke his heart so badly, left his future looking grim.

Then friends began to vanish, some to distance, some to time,
Some to choices that diverged, some to Death's relentless climb,
He'd scroll through social media, see the faces that were gone,
Wonder why he couldn't keep them, what he'd said or done wrong,
The funerals came too frequent, the silence grew too loud,
Baby Fluff collected losses like storm clouds gather in a shroud.

The darkness crept in slowly, then it flooded all at once,
Depression wrapped around him like a coat he wore for months,
Every morning felt like drowning, every night felt twice as long,
The world became a distant place where he just didn't belong,
His mind became a battlefield, where thoughts attacked like a fighter plane,
Baby Fluff fought just to make it through, slowly going insane.

He'd smile and say "I'm doing well," when asked by those who cared,
But inside he was collapsing, too ashamed to say he's scared.
Knowledge gathered over years, trying to understand his pain,
He finally figured out why the thoughts that danced inside his brain,
Moved to a different tune from others, saw patterns that others miss,
And suddenly his lifetime of confusion started making sense like this.

Why crowds and noise felt overwhelming, why small talk drained him dry,
Why he'd lose hours to his passions, let the whole world pass him by,
Why changes threw him off balance, why he needed structure's frame,
Why eye contact felt uncomfortable, why friendship felt like game,
An expert later confirmed it, gave these patterns neurodivergent names,
Understanding didn't cure them, but it validated all his claims.

But knowing wasn't fixing, and the darkness still held sway,
Until something deep inside him whispered "Not today,"
A spark of stubborn anger, a refusal to give in,
He decided if he's fighting, then he's damn well going to win,
Started working on himself, one tiny step at a time,
Baby Fluff discovered something: he could learn to climb.

His friends saw him writing once, the words he'd been too scared to share,
"The world needs to hear these words," they said with genuine care,
"You're not the only one who's felt this specific kind of pain,
Your verses could be someone's lighthouse in their hurricane,
Tell your story through your poems, make them into something real,
Turn your private wounds public, help the broken start to heal."

So here he sits, a 90s baby, grown up and still alive,
Compiling all his scattered thoughts, with a zealous drive,
Crafting words from his pain, turning his struggles into song,
Baby Fluff decided he would put his words where they belong,
This story that you're drinking in, is proof he made it through,
And if he could survive his storms, then surely so can you.

So what did Baby Fluff learn from the gauntlet he survived?
That making it this far means that he will continue to thrive,
The battles didn't break him, though they bent him pretty hard,
Each struggle was a teacher, each wound left a teaching scar,
He's stronger than he realized, far tougher than he knew,
The darkness tried to claim him, but he fought his way back through.

He learned that growth requires risk, demands you step outside,
The comfort zone that feels so safe becomes the place dreams died,
You can't discover who you are by staying where you've been,
The person he's becoming needs the courage to begin,
To try and fail and try again, to stumble and to fall,
Because playing it safe forever means you never lived at all.

He learned that vulnerability isn't weakness, it's his strength,
That showing up authentically, going to any length,
To share his truth and bare his soul took more courage than to hide,
The tales that he was too scared to show became his greatest pride,
Pretending to be okay just kept him lonely, pulling sadness in tow,
But owning all his broken parts has helped his garden grow.

He learned his worth was never tied to what the others thought,
That validation from outside was a battle always fought,
And never truly won because opinions always shift,
The only voice that matters is the one that gives the gift,
Of self-acceptance, self-compassion, with grace that does bless,
Baby Fluff stopped asking "Am I worthy?" – realized the answer was "Yes"

He learned that pain has purpose, though it's hard to see it through,
The struggles weren't just random, they were sculpting something new,
A person who could empathize, who understood the fight,
Who'd been through hell and back again and still chose to find light,
He wouldn't erase the hard parts even if he somehow could,
Because it would be like removing the engine from under a car's hood.

He's looking to the future now with hope instead of dread,
Still healing, still growing, still rewiring what's in his head,
Not trying to be perfect, just committed to improve,
To better himself daily, find his rhythm and his groove,
The past taught him lessons, but it doesn't own his fate,
Baby Fluff's discovering his own story now – it's never too late.

And here's what he believes now, standing on the other side,
That he's allowed to be both broken and still filled with pride,
A masterpiece and work in progress, simultaneously both,
That healing isn't linear, it's a journey of slow growth,
He's grateful for the hands who held him, helped him fight his dread,
Now Baby Fluff can write the chapters he once thought would be left unread.

Now let me speak to you directly, the person reading or hearing this,
If you're feeling broken, lost, or trapped inside the abyss,
Know that you're not alone in this, we've walked these paths before,
Every person you admire has fought their private war,
Your pain is valid, real, and true, your struggle matters here,
And the fact you're still breathing proves you're stronger than your fear.

You don't need to have it figured out, don't need a perfect plan,
You're allowed to ask for help, to stumble, fall, and barely stand,
Your timeline isn't anyone's but yours alone to write,
Comparison will steal your joy and dim your inner light,
Stop measuring your chapter one against their chapter ten,
Your story's still unfolding – give yourself time to write it, friend.

You're braver than you believe right now, stronger than you feel,
The world needs your unique story, needs you to voice what's real,
Don't wait for someone's permission to exist, create, or shine,
Don't let the fear of judgment keep your brilliance in decline,
You matter just by being here, your presence is enough,
Your existence is your birthright, just like it was for Baby Fluff.

We're all some version of that kid, just wearing different skin,
Wrong-shaped pieces wondering where we're supposed to fit in,
But here's the secret that he learned through all his darkest nights,
It's never too late to believe in yourself, to claim what are your rights,
To say "I'm worth the effort, worth the healing, worth the try,"
To pick yourself back up again each time you wonder why.

Learn from your experiences but don't let them define,
Your past is not your prison, it's the soil where you'll refine,
The person you're becoming through the trials you endure,
Write your own story, even when the ending seems unsure,
Be gentle with yourself, you're doing better than you know,
You're tending to your garden, even when it's hard to grow.

So here we stand together as this story finds its end,
But Baby Fluff's still writing, there are pages yet to pen,
His story isn't finished, and neither, my friend, is yours,
This ending is a beginning, opening brand new doors,
We've walked through the night, fought our fears head on,
From darkness to dawn, with our dreams – the journey carries on.

The End
Hi, I'm
Baby Fluff

Or is it
?
Hi, I'm
Baby Fluff

ABOUT THE AUTHOR

Mohak Suri is a 90s kid who was born in New Delhi, India. Shaped by a childhood before constant connectivity and an adulthood defined by it, he writes from the heart giving shape to his life experiences by putting them into words.

'Musings of a 90s Baby' is his first published poetry collection.

He is the "Baby Fluff" from the final piece of this book, known to friends by the nickname "Fluffy" since 2006.